GW01398766

Original Title: Betrayed

Editors: Theodor Taimla
Autor: Anett Arumets
ISBN 978-9916-756-16-4

Betrayed

Anett Arumets

Silent Rupture

In the stillness of the night,
Quiet battles we must fight.
Words unspoken, hearts in flight,
Trust reduced to mere twilight.

Dreams once shared now lie in shreds,
Secrets whispered, tangled threads.
In the silence, pain embeds,
Lonely nights on tear-stained beds.

The Backstabber's Tale

Lies concealed in friendly guise,
Hollow laughter, hidden sighs.
Truth obscured by cunning eyes,
Betrayal's shadow never lies.

Once a friend, now cloaked in spite,
Twisted paths where dark meets light.
Behind the mask, a bitter bite,
Trust deformed in deceit's blight.

Veil of Treachery

Beneath the veil, a truth unknown,
Whispers carried, seeds are sown.
Masks of trust are overthrown,
Leaves the soul to stand alone.

In shadows deep, the lies unfold,
Stories twisted, faith is sold.
Hearts once warm, now dark and cold,
Trust, a tale no longer told.

Faith's Demise

Once we held a dream so bright,
Vanished now, like stars in night.
Promises turned into plight,
Faith abandoned in its flight.

Hope once woven, deeply tied,
Truth now fractured, dreams denied.
In the wreckage, love has died,
Faith's demise, our hearts have cried.

Hollow Assurance

Promises wrapped in dusk's allure,
Whispers fade, none endure.
Echoes of what might have been,
Lost within the evening's sheen.

Words once held so firm and tight,
Now mere shadows in the night.
Trust once golden, now a trace,
Fleeting as the moon's embrace.

Dreams dissolve in twilight's grace,
Leaves no mark, leaves no trace.
Vows dissolve like morning dew,
Out of sight, out of view.

Brittle Allegiance

Pledges bound in thinest thread,
Fragile as the words once said.
Loyalty a fleeting breath,
Waning with each silent step.

Unseen fractures, hidden flaw,
In the silent broken law.
Trust cascading in despair,
Cracks revealed, none repair.

Hearts once welded, now in drift,
Adrift in time's cruel swift.
Truths forsaken, bonds unwound,
In the shadows, lost and found.

Sundered Hearts

Lovers once in perfect sync,
Now on edges, backs to brink.
Silent screams and muffled cries,
Echoes of our last goodbyes.

Promises now turned to dust,
Wings clipped of a summer's trust.
Cold lips meet with hollow kiss,
What was ours, we won't miss.

Memories now split in two,
Tears dried on what's left of you.
Sundered hearts, the final mark,
Lost beneath the sky so dark.

The Judas Touch

Treachery beneath the skin,
Smiling face, deceit within.
Golden heart that turned to lead,
In the shadow's twisting thread.

Trust betrayed by silent glance,
Fortune lost in fleeting chance.
Hands that once were clasped in faith,
Now undone by whispered wraith.

Scars remain behind the smile,
Tales of truth wrapped in guile.
Each touch a curse, a hollow friend,
Judas knows how stories end.

The Deceiver's Smile

Behind lips that softly curve,
Lies a heart with tricks and nerve.
Promises fade in a while,
Masked beneath the deceiver's smile.

Words like honey, sweet and sly,
Cast illusions, questions why.
Trust in shambles, hearts defiled,
Lost within the deceiver's smile.

Mirth and malice intertwined,
Anguish follows in their mind.
Feelings twisted, thoughts beguiled,
Waning from the deceiver's smile.

Truths Unraveled

Hidden layers, core revealed,
Wounds so deep that never healed.
Voices in the dark, disheveled,
Secrets whisper, truths unraveled.

Lies once scattered fade away,
Night gives in to welcome day.
Shadows of deceit, disheveled,
Vanquished by truths unraveled.

Clarity, a beacon bright,
Pierces through the darkest night.
No more webs of lies bedeviled,
Peace at last, truths unraveled.

Forsaken Pledge

Promises, like morning dew,
Vanish with the sunlight's view.
Words once spoken, heartstrings dredged,
Now remain a forsaken pledge.

Vows forgotten, bonds unmade,
Echoes of the love that swayed.
Silent whispers, dreams abridged,
Crumbled by a forsaken pledge.

Eyes that once beheld the dawn,
Now reflect a love withdrawn.
In the void where love once edged,
Lingers still a forsaken pledge.

Shadows of Betrayal

In the dark where secrets lie,
Trust is broken, shadows fly.
Beneath the facade, fragile and frail,
Lurk the echoes of betrayal.

Eyes that wander, hearts that stray,
Blinded by a cruel array.
Innocence lost in sorrow's scale,
Haunted by the shadows of betrayal.

Once pure bonds now turned to dust,
Promises eroded, lost in lust.
In the silence, voices wail,
Echoes of the shadows of betrayal.

Broken Bonds

Threads once woven, now frayed and torn,
Silent echoes of the love we mourn.
Promises shattered, scattered like leaves,
In the cold wind that never grieves.

Eyes once bright, now dimmed by time,
Hearts that forgot their synchronized rhyme.
Footsteps diverge on paths unknown,
Leaving shadows where trust was sown.

Memories linger, ghosts of the past,
Whispered secrets, fading fast.
Yet in the ruins, new hopes bloom,
Rising from the deepest gloom.

Stolen Truths

Words once pure, now tainted lies,
Veils drawn over innocent eyes.
The truth, once lost, remains a ghost,
Haunting the halls we cherished most.

Shadows dance where light once played,
Trust eroded, sweet dreams betrayed.
In the mirror, reflections break,
Revealing the masks we all forsake.

In the silence, secrets seep,
Wounds too deep for time to keep.
Yet from the ashes, tales unfold,
Of courage new and spirits bold.

Illusion's End

Mirages fade as dawn finds its way,
Truth emerges in the light of day.
Promises dissolve like morning mist,
Revealing lies that once persist.

Eyes awaken to the stark reveal,
Beneath the surface, truths congeal.
In falsehood's wake, clarity blooms,
Dispelling shadows, brightening rooms.

In broken mirrors, truths we find,
New perspectives, untangled mind.
Tho' illusions fall, hope ascends,
In the dawning light of illusion's end.

Facade's Collapse

Walls painted with smiling lies,
Crumble under truthful skies.
Pretenses fall, masks unwind,
Revealing scars we sought to hide.

In the rubble of deceit's nest,
Fragile truth now stands confessed.
Faces bare, we start anew,
With hearts revealed, dangers few.

Through the chaos, silence speaks,
Of broken fronts and humble peaks.
Rebuilding trust on shattered ground,
With honesty's pure, untainted sound.

Trust's Abyss

In shadows deep, trust takes its fall,
A whispered doubt, the silent call.
Through night's veil, the secrets twine,
Lost in the dark, a fractured line.

Eyes once bright now cast away,
A hidden truth in light of day.
The heart's chasm, a void so grand,
Trust's abyss, a desolate land.

Promises fade like mists at dawn,
Barely seen, forever gone.
Faith in others, now astray,
A silent echo in dismay.

The Unseen Rift

In quiet tones, the discord spreads,
Between us now, the silence spreads.
Words unspoken, gaps unfelt,
The unseen rift where heartbreak dwelt.

Eyes averted, paths diverge,
Unshed tears on the verge.
Once together, now apart,
An unseen rift, a broken heart.

What once was whole, now split in two,
An endless void, me and you.
Bridges burned, the air now swift,
The lingering pain of the unseen rift.

Poisoned Words

Sharp as knives, the words take flight,
In shadows lurk, out of sight.
Tongues like venom, hearts now scarred,
Poisoned words, defenses marred.

Trust eroded, broken apart,
Every syllable, a piercing dart.
Whispers cold, lies entwined,
Poisoned words, intent designed.

Friend turned foe, the pain instilled,
With each utterance, a bond is killed.
The toxin spreads, love becomes blurred,
The haunting echo of poisoned words.

The Fading Bond

Tethers strained, frayed and worn,
Memories of a love now torn.
A bond once strong now fades away,
Slip through fingers like a day's ray.

Laughter echoes in hollow halls,
Echo of love, the silence calls.
Eyes once met with shared delight,
Now turn away, avoid the light.

Time has worn the ties that bind,
In the past, a love confined.
The fading bond, a silent song,
A whisper of where we once belonged.

Shattered Promises

Beneath the moon's pale, ghostly light,
Whispers of a night gone cold.
Echoes of our vows, once bright,
Now lie broken, stories untold.

Dreams we wove with threads of gold,
Lie in shards upon the ground.
Promises we could not hold,
Lost in time, no longer found.

In the stillness, shadows dance,
Mock reflections of our past.
Fate has severed our romance,
Left in fragments, fate so vast.

Tears that glistened on your cheek,
Fall like stars from trails above.
Silent cries, our hearts now weak,
Shattered promises of love.

In the quiet of this night,
Memories in fragments lay.
Broken dreams have taken flight,
As shattered promises fade away.

The Empty Embrace

In the silence of the night,
Lies an echo of our pain.
Once we held each other tight,
Now we're strangers in the rain.

Once a warmth that lit the dark,
Now a shadow takes its place.
Eyes that held a lover's spark,
Now reflect an empty space.

Hands that once were intertwined,
Now are cold and far apart.
Memories we cannot find,
Leave a void within the heart.

Whispers lost upon the air,
Barely reach the distant shore.
In the void, there's no repair,
For the love we had before.

In this cold and vacant place,
Hopes and dreams are laid to waste.
All that's left, an empty embrace,
Of a love that time erased.

Love's Mirage

In the desert of my soul, you came,
An oasis I could see.
Mirrored glimmers, love aflame,
Fading quick like morning's glee.

Dreams that sparkled in the heat,
Promises of cool, soft rain.
Winds that whispered bittersweet,
Chasing shadows, leaving pain.

Illusions danced within our grasp,
Mirages both near and far.
Hope slipped through our fingers' clasp,
Like the light of evening star.

Parched beneath the burning sun,
We sought refuge in love's name.
But the journey's far from done,
Only thirst and fleeting game.

In the end, we're left alone,
Chasing dreams that fade away.
Love's mirage, a fleeting tone,
Lost within the light of day.

Cracked Foundation

Upon our home, lies shattered ground,
Cracks that spread with time's cruel hand.
Once firm walls now won't rebound,
Tremors shake our heart's command.

Love that stood like granite stone,
Now is fractured, failing fast.
Promises become cold stoned,
Dreams we built are of the past.

Every whispered sigh and tear,
Eroded trust, its grip unfast.
Cracks revealed our silent fear,
Built on faults that couldn't last.

Echoes in the empty rooms,
Speak of times we thought were true.
Now they loom like distant tombs,
Memories that bid adieu.

Though the walls may still remain,
Foundations crumble, break apart.
Love we thought would overcome,
Wears away with every heart.

The Diverging Path

At the fork the road divides
Into realms unknown and vast
One path winds through gentle tides
The other shadows from the past

Step by step, the journey goes
Choices made, the future sealed
In each twist, a secret shows
What fate's hand has yet revealed

Sunlit fields or stormy gales
Fortunes change with every turn
In mute tales, the gravel trails
Speak of lessons we must learn

Onward through the moss and stone
With hearts as guides, and eyes as lights
Paths may wander, lead alone
But courage fuels the darkest nights

Thus we walk, the road unfold
In diverging paths we trust
With each step, the stories told
Of our dreams turned into dust

Cloaked Treachery

Behind the smile, a shadow rests
Eyes that glint with hidden guile
Whispers masked in jestful quests
Veiling hearts with cunning style

Intentions wrapped in silken lies
A masquerade of trust and cheer
Beneath the laughter, plotters rise
Drawing close with fabled fear

In moonlit halls where secrets creep
A roguish hand dismantles trust
Promises, like brittle leaves
Crushed beneath the weight of lust

Vows exchanged in twilight's haze
Deception haunts each edge and seam
Treachery in cloaked arrays
Turns love into a fleeting dream

Yet through the mask, a truth resides
That light can pierce the darkest veil
Even cloaked in deceit's tides
Integrity shall still prevail

The Phantom Trust

Invisible bonds, unseen threads
Connecting souls through time's great flow
A trust that's born where no one treads
In shadows where true friendships grow

Ghostly whispers carried far
Promises forged, yet never heard
Emotions bright as northern star
Invisible, in quiet word

In the silence, stories blend
Of faith unspoken, trust sustained
Between the lines, where acts intend
A binding trust, so unconstrained

Through trials where our spirits bend
Where doubts roil like stormy seas
Trust endures as unseen friend
Phantom roots of forest trees

Though unseen, the bond remains
A spectral cord in twilight's mist
Trust persists through joys and pains
An eternal, unseen tryst

Ghosts of Truth

In the quiet, truth does creep
Haunting halls where secrets lie
Silent phantoms, they shall seep
Through the veil of each denied

Shadows dance, where lies decay
Echoes of forgotten word
Memories of a distant day
In the whispers often heard

Revelations veiled in grey
Surfaced in a shrouded breath
Ghosts of truth will find their way
Through the silent walls of death

Barefaced moments of the past
Rise like specters in the haze
Fleeting glimpses, shadows cast
On life's intricate displays

In those ghosts, the truth resides
Uncovered through the time and dust
Despite the cloak of many hides
It surfaces, because it must

Veil of Lies

Behind your smile, a shadow lies
A whispered truth that softly dies
In tangled words, the secrets dwell
Within the heart, their poison swell

Your gaze so clear, deceiving art
Each look another fractured part
The veiled disguise, so sweetly draped
My trust ensnared, forever taped

A fleeting glance, a silent tear
The hidden shame I do not hear
For every lie, a thread is spun
Till webs betray the morning sun

Yet in your eyes, a tale untold
Of warmth that withers into cold
Behind your mask, the sorrow sighs
A haunted dance in veil of lies

Crimson Promises

In twilight's glow, our oaths were made
Beneath the sky, as dusk did fade
A pledge of love, so bright and bold
In crimson promises, hearts unfold

Yet time does drift, and shadows creep
The vows we swore, now buried deep
Silent echoes in the night
Of promises once shining bright

Our hands did clasp, with hearts aflame
Yet words do falter, love the same
The crimson hue of twilight's kiss
A memory that we do miss

Though worlds apart, our hearts remain
In whispered thoughts, the love, the pain
For crimson promises, once true
Now linger in the morning dew

Silent Treachery

In quiet hours, the demons play
Through silent whispers, night and day
Their stealthy touch, a creeping dread
Through dreams undone, and words unsaid

A friend's embrace, a stranger's blade
In shadows deep, the trust does fade
The silent treachery so grand
A coward's art, so deftly planned

A lie in wait, the trap concealed
The silent treachery revealed
A dagger poised, a secret thrust
In bitter hearts, the seeds of rust

Yet still within, the strength to rise
To meet deceit with clearer eyes
For in the dark, a truth to see
Beyond the silent treachery

Splintered Dreams

In midnight's hush, the dreams do break
A fragile wish, the heart forsake
The splintered dreams, a fleeting sigh
Of hopes that fade as night goes by

Each shard reflects the light once known
A fractured past, a future flown
In shadowed depths, the echoes ring
Of dreams once whole, now lost to sting

In every tear, a dreamlet sprawls
Upon the ground, the silent calls
Of yearning hearts, the broken beams
The silent wail of splintered dreams

Yet in the dawn, a fragile ray
A chance to mend, a path to sway
For splintered dreams may find relief
In morning's light, a kinder grief

The Judas Kiss

In shadows, where secrets lie
A kiss betrays the night
Whispers of lost trust sigh
Under pale, deceitful light

A moment, forever stained
With treachery's cruel kiss
Friendship, now unchained
To a dark, abyssal abyss

Love turned to bitter grief
With just one transient touch
Faith shattered, beyond belief
Left longing in its clutch

Beneath the moon's cold gaze
The heart knows well its loss
In passion's silent blaze
Trust burns, and lines are crossed

A Judas kiss, so cold
Betrayal's tender mark
Stories of love retold
In shadows, deep and stark

Promises in Ash

Once whispered vows ignite
In the heat of fervent flame
Dreams, so pure and bright
Left only ashen, name

Love's bonfire burns so fierce
Breath of lies fuels the blaze
Emotion's truth, it pierces
In passion's frenzied daze

Memories, in smoke they rise
Promises crumble, fall
Tears trace mournful skies
Empty echoes call

Heartbeats count the cost
Of dreams reduced to dust
Time's innocence, now lost
In betrayal's dark thrust

Ashes of hope remain
In love's deserted land
Caught in sorrow's reign
On grief's shifting sand

Erased Fidelity

Once woven, threads of gold
Bind hearts, so strong and true
Loyalty we boldly hold
Yet vanish like the dew

Promises, now shadows
Of love once held so dear
Trust drowned in sorrow's throes
Faith erased by fear

Bonds break, as whispers fade
Truth hidden in disdain
In memory's bitter shade
Painful ghosts remain

Void of love's embrace
Fidelity, dissolved
In betrayal's empty space
Mysteries revolve

Hearts, like pages torn
From the book of yesterday
In faith's quiet scorn
Lost words fade away

Blades of Deceit

Deception's knife so keen
Cuts deep where trust once lay
In fields of shattered dreams
The heart's dear truths betray

Blades of deceit, they gleam
Under moon's cold stare
In the wake of vanished dreams
Lies whisper in the air

Eyes once warm, turn cold
Fractures in the soul
Stories of love retold
In hollow, empty role

Trust, a fragile glass
Broken by deceit's hand
Shards of the love that was
Scattered on barren land

From dawn till dusk, it seeps
This pain, so bittersweet
In the garden, sorrow weeps
'Neath blades of cold deceit

Shattered Trust

Beneath the moon's pale glow,
Promises once firm now lie,
In fragments scattered low,
Love sworn turns to sigh.

A bond once strong, now frail,
Winds of doubt do gust,
In heart's chamber, it does wail,
Lost is our mutual trust.

Echoes of our laughter,
Fade to whispers, faint,
Truths that came hereafter,
Left all pure hearts taint.

Shadows cloak our memories,
A chill within love's past,
From warm, bright histories,
To cold moments that last.

Though the sun may rise again,
A scarred heart's slow to mend,
Shattered trust became our bane,
Love's fragile, bitter end.

Whispers in the Dark

Midnight's cloak, a silent veil,
Secrets spoken, frail yet stark,
Truth hidden in the tale,
Of whispers in the dark.

Stars listen, distant eyes,
To murmurs soft, we can't deny,
In shadows where our spirit lies,
Dark whispers pass us by.

Moonlight casts an eerie glow,
On voices that the silence break,
Silken threads of unseen woe,
Drip secrets in their wake.

Hearts encased in shadow's shroud,
List to tones they can't unhear,
In twilight's grasp, so proud,
They whisper every fear.

Bound by night, these hushed confides,
In silent dark, they starkly mark,
Echoes heard where truth abides,
From whispers in the dark.

Fractured Vows

Once solemnly spoken,
Words that bound us strong,
Now those vows are broken,
Their melody a wrong.

Ring placed with tender hand,
Promises seemed eternal,
Built our love on shifting sand,
Now all seems infernal.

Eyes once filled with honor,
Now cast shadows of dismay,
In the mirror, a mourner,
Reflects a love that sways.

Petals of our shared bouquet,
Scattered by a gale,
Beneath the storm they lay,
As fractured vows set sail.

Silent sobs of what's destroyed,
In the heart's silent muse,
Fractured vows leave a void,
On paths we did not choose.

Echoes of Deception

In the hollow of night,
Where shadows come to play,
Echoes of deception,
Lead innocence astray.

Masked by friendly smiles,
Yet words with subtle knives,
Carve out in many wiles,
Truth wanes, deceit thrives.

Once trusting heart now guarded,
Against the whispers sly,
A mind once open-hearted,
Shuts down as trust runs dry.

Veils of treachery fall,
To show what lies within,
Behind each painted wall,
Deception's cruel grin.

Through tangled webs we've weaved,
Truth tangled in perception,
In silence, we perceived,
Echoes of deception.

Veil of Falsehood

Whispers cloaked in shadows rise,
Behind bright eyes, deceit is spun.
Truth concealed in crafted lies,
Moonlight fades before the sun.

Promises like gauze so thin,
Yet bind the heart in webs untrue.
Secrets sowed beneath the skin,
A mask worn tight, a hidden clue.

Hope entwined with false pretense,
Trust betrayed by subtle art.
Veil of falsehood, cruel defense,
Hiding treachery in the heart.

Echoes of forgotten dreams,
Dancing on the brink of night.
Where nothing's ever as it seems,
Behind the veil, the truth takes flight.

Illusions crafted to deceive,
Lost in shadows, hope remains.
In falsehood's grip, we interweave,
A tapestry of hidden pains.

The Unseen Knife

In the silence, danger lurks,
Hidden blade with deadly aim.
Trust is shattered, madness smirks,
Wounds inflicted without name.

Friendship's blade betrays unseen,
Cuts the heart with stealthy stroke.
Venomous and so serene,
Turns the bond to bitter smoke.

Promises dissolve to dust,
When the unseen knife takes flight.
Carving deep the bond of trust,
Bringing shadows to the light.

Fear embeds within the mind,
Of the cut that's unforeseen.
In the dark, intentions blind,
Sharper still than edges keen.

Hope retreats, as night proceeds,
Underneath the cloak of dark.
Unseen knife and hidden deeds,
Leave within an aching mark.

Misguided Faith

Faith misplaced, a trust so blind,
Wandering the misguided path.
Seeking solace, none will find,
Lost within the tempest's wrath.

Promises of light ahead,
Illusions of a golden dawn.
Following where angels tread,
Yet led astray by false foregone.

Belief entwined with empty words,
Chasing shadows in the dark.
Hope unlike the soaring birds,
Tethered close to fleeting spark.

Misguided faith, a fragile thing,
That bends and breaks under deceit.
Trust once blooming in the spring,
Now wilted by the summer heat.

Lessons learned in bitter night,
Where deceptions find their place.
Misguided faith, a dimming light,
Leaving scars upon the face.

Illusions of Sincerity

Glimmers of sincerity,
Shining in the false veneer.
Masked behind complexity,
True intentions disappear.

Gentle words with hardened core,
Soft caresses hiding steel.
Illusions built on trusty floor,
Only to conceal and steal.

Tender touch, with practiced grace,
Crafted guise to beguile the heart.
Hidden truths in plainest face,
Perfidy, a subtle art.

Trust bestowed on fragile guise,
Tumbling down like autumn leaves.
In the web of crafted lies,
Truth beneath deceit now weaves.

Sincerity, a fleeting dream,
Illusions spun with utmost care.
Unraveling at hidden seam,
Revealing falsehood in the glare.

The Double-Edged Smile

A smile so bright, it hides the thorn,
Underneath, intentions worn,
The sweetest charm, with edges frayed,
Within the light, the shadows played.

A friendly face, a gentle guise,
Behind the mask, deceit lies,
In trust, the venom softly seeps,
Within the smile, betrayal sleeps.

Among the crowd, a shining pearl,
A twist of fate, a twirling whirl,
The double edge, both sharp and sly,
In mirth concealed, the subtle lie.

Bright as dawn, the gesture warm,
Yet storms can stir within this form,
The subtle curve can twist the tale,
Beneath the smile, truths often pale.

In eyes that sparkle, truth can fade,
As trust and doubt play masquerade,
The double-edged smile, a perilous art,
A blade that cuts both heart and heart.

Disguised in Friendship

In friendship's cloak, intent confound,
Hidden whispers make no sound,
A touch sincere, a glance so kind,
Yet shadows drift within the mind.

Through laughter shared and smiles bright,
Lurks secrets born in darkest night,
A hand to hold, a guiding light,
But trust can wane, from gentle spite.

In close embrace, the world seems clear,
Yet close the ear for whispers near,
Where alliances fade, divergence starts,
Disguised in friendship, silent darts.

In moments grand, in bonds so tight,
Lies masked resentments out of sight,
In truth and jest, the lines can blur,
In friendship's guise, the lies transfer.

A word of cheer, a heart so near,
Yet trust can shatter, year by year,
Disguised in friendship, wounds may heal,
But scars reveal what hearts conceal.

The Unraveled Bond

At first, the weave, the braid so tight,
A bond unraveled by the night,
In daylight's beam, the cords were bound,
Yet shadows twist, and threads unwound.

Once interlaced in perfect form,
Through tempests, kept each other warm,
But time reveals the hidden fray,
As bonds once strong begin to sway.

The trust that held, now starts to break,
Each tender word begins to quake,
In moments keen, and silence grown,
The space between, so keenly sown.

A whisper, then, a pull, a tear,
An empty void starts growing there,
What once was close, now drifts apart,
The bond unraveled, heart from heart.

In memories, the echoes stay,
Of bonds that time could not delay,
Yet in the end, the truth is stark,
An unraveled bond leaves a lasting mark.

False Witness

In shadowed halls, the whispers crept,
A false witness, dark secrets kept,
In silent courts, where truth was swayed,
The lies took root, the trust decayed.

A gaze so firm, yet built on lies,
A truth obscured, beneath disguise,
A claim so bold, yet so untrue,
In falsehood's grasp, the doubt then grew.

In testimony, firm and clear,
Crafted well to stoke the fear,
The words of trust, now brittle glass,
A shatter with each uttered pass.

Yet justice hides beneath the veil,
Seeking truth where lies prevail,
In witnesses with hearts so cold,
The falsehoods crafted, stories bold.

But time will carve the truth in stone,
Expose the lies once brightly shone,
False witness may deceive the eye,
Yet time will strip the truth from lie.

Shadows in Trust

In twilight's gentle, muted form,
Where silent whispers softly storm,
A trust once firm, now shades betray,
In shadowed eves, we lose our way.

Cold, is the dusk when trust is lost,
A bitter chill, a heavy cost,
Echoes fading in the dim,
Where hopes once bright, now shadows swim.

A glance, a touch, yet hearts are wary,
In hidden doubts, our burdens carry,
The moon, a silent witness stands,
To fragile dreams, now grains of sand.

Beneath the stars, reflections dance,
Of broken bonds and lost romance,
Yet in the night, a seed is sown,
In trust's return, a light is shown.

The Broken Vows

In sunlit halls where vows were made,
Our promises, as gold, we laid,
Yet time has worn, and shadows creep,
In hearts, once pure, the silence seep.

A touch, a sigh, a turning glance,
The music fades, no more the dance,
A cruel betrayal, whispers cold,
The bonds of trust, now lost, untold.

Yearning eyes and empty hands,
The future's path, like shifting sands,
Words once strong, now frail as dust,
Love's sacred vow, betrayed by lust.

Yet in the tear, the heart release,
A tender hope, for silent peace,
Though vows are broken, hearts may mend,
In time, all wounds, the nights will tend.

Echoes of Lies

In echoes past, the truth was veiled,
Where lies were spun, and hearts derailed,
A mask was worn, with eyes so bold,
Yet underneath, the shadows told.

A whisper here, a secret there,
The tangled web, so fine and rare,
In darkness deep, the truth concealed,
Yet in the end, all hearts revealed.

The promises, within a shade,
Each word a dagger, finely made,
In echoes found, the silence cries,
A history of hidden lies.

Yet even lies, though darkness thrives,
Cannot crush, where light survives,
For in the end, the dawn will break,
And heart's true song, will silence ache.

Silent Tears

The dawn arises, pale and cold,
With silent tears, our tale unfold,
The hopes we had, now turned to dust,
In shadows deep, no longer trust.

A sigh, a pause, a broken sound,
Where once our laughter did abound,
The silent tears, like gentle rain,
Mark the scars of hidden pain.

In quiet nights, the memories stay,
Of times when love was clear as day,
Yet now in whispers, softly call,
The echoes of a distant fall.

And though the tears may gently flow,
Within the night, the heart will grow,
A strength emerges, soft yet clear,
In silent tears, salvation near.

The Hollow Pledge

Promises made beneath the moon,
Vanished like the morning dew,
Whispers echo in the gloom,
Shadows where once light was true.

The stars bear silent witness,
To vows that turned to dust,
Lovers bound by bliss,
Betrayed by broken trust.

Empty words like autumn leaves,
Drift away on winds of time,
What remains of gentle eves,
Lost to life's unspoken crime.

Echoes faint of laughter sweet,
Haunt the halls of yesteryears,
Steps retraced by weary feet,
Marked by silent, fleeting tears.

Oh, the weight of empty vows,
Cast aside in fleeting haste,
Life resumes, but sorrow plows,
Fields once rich, laid now to waste.

Secrets Unveiled

Beneath the cloak of midnight,
Whispers dance on the breeze,
Hidden truths in soft moonlight,
A mystery that teases.

Eyes that see beyond the veil,
Reflections in the glass,
Tales of old must not fail,
But the truth can't help but pass.

Candles flicker, shadows loom,
Revealing what they must,
In the silence of the room,
Confidences earn our trust.

Mirrors cracked by knowledge gained,
No longer can deceive,
Every whisper, every stain,
Now permission to believe.

In the twilight of our dreams,
Secrets we once held tight,
Unravel like ancient seams,
Exposing all to sight.

The Stolen Heart

In the quiet of the night,
A thief with gentle hands,
Took a heart, left no slight,
Love's map with tender plans.

Eyes that spoke of yearning,
Silent pleas for grace,
Souls like stars, brightly burning,
In an intimate embrace.

Caught in webs of affection,
Entangled in a gaze,
Love's path, a new direction,
Lost within a daze.

Whispered vows, like secrets,
Stolen in the dark,
Bound by love's sweet precepts,
Embarked without a mark.

Hearts entwined, forevermore,
By fate's unwritten chart,
What was lost, now restored,
In the tale of the stolen heart.

Hidden Agendas

Faces masked in twilight,
Plans concealed in time,
In shadows of the moonlight,
Lies of grand design.

Beneath each smile, a story,
Unseen by honest eyes,
A quest for hidden glory,
Played under the guise.

Words as delicate as flowers,
Hide intentions deep,
Power weaves through hours,
Secrets ours to keep.

Eyes that see beneath,
The layers of pretense,
Unraveling what's beneath,
The cloak of false defense.

When dawn returns the light,
And shadows softly fade,
Hidden agendas bright,
In truth we are remade.

Veins of Betrayal

In shadows deep, where trust did fade,
A friendship old by lies mislaid,
Veins of betrayal, dark and cold,
A silent pain in secrets told.

The bond we shared, now shattered glass,
Reflections of a tarnished past,
Through whispered winds, the truth unveiled,
A soul's great wound, no word can hail.

An open heart, once pure and bright,
Now tangled in the webs of night,
For every smile that masked the stain,
In veins of betrayal flows the pain.

Your eyes once kind, now bear the mark,
Of shadows cast within the dark,
While tears fall soft on broken ground,
The echoes of deceit resound.

In reverie of days now gone,
A trust betrayed, a friendship pawned,
Yet through the sorrow's endless sway,
The strength to heal shall find its way.

The Traitor's Whisper

Beneath the moon's cold, watchful eye,
There drift the whispers, soft yet sly,
The traitor's voice, a serpent's hiss,
A broken trust in twilight's kiss.

Once loyal words, now drenched in frost,
In memories of friendships lost,
The whisper winds, through tangled past,
An anguish that shall ever last.

In shadows long, their ghostly form,
The traitor's soul, a twisted storm,
Through corridors of doubt they roam,
Their whisper haunting, far from home.

The heart once warm, now wrought in steel,
Forbidden truth, too harsh to feel,
For every whisper, every breath,
Resounds the traitor's loyal death.

Yet through the dark, the dawn shall break,
A dawn of light for healing's sake,
Though whispers stay, like ancient scars,
New bonds shall shine like morning stars.

Fallen Loyalty

From highest heights, the fall began,
Where loyalty was once our plan,
A friendship forged in trust and steel,
Now broken wings and wounds unhealed.

In gardens where our laughter bloomed,
The shadow's seeds of doubt consumed,
Fallen loyalty, the price unknown,
In hearts where faith was freely sown.

With every promise made in light,
Now buried in the darkest night,
Beneath the stars that once did gleam,
Lies shattered hope and broken dream.

The echoes of a loyal past,
Now whisper winds of change so fast,
As roots once deep, now twisted dry,
In fallen trust, our spirits cry.

Yet through the ashes, embers glow,
In time, a strength anew shall grow,
For loyalty, though once betrayed,
Within new bonds shall be remade.

Echoes of Falsehood

In the chambers of the heart's delight,
Where truth was meant to conquer night,
Echoes of falsehood, soft and sly,
Through broken dreams their whispers fly.

Once words of gold, now turned to dust,
In twilight's glow, a shattered trust,
The echoes dance on winds of change,
Within the heart, a hidden range.

Deceptions weave through time and space,
In shadows long, they leave their trace,
With every lie, a tether breaks,
In echoes, bitter truth awakes.

The canvas painted, now undone,
A friendship lost, a battle won,
Yet through the echoes, silent wane,
A voice of truth shall rise again.

For every falsehood deeply sown,
A seed of strength within is grown,
And though the echoes softly lie,
The heart shall mend, and reach the sky.

Anchors Adrift

Anchors once steadfast, now adrift,
Boundless seas, they start to shift.
Ties that held in stormy gales,
Now lose grip as courage pales.

Forever known, the steadfast chain,
Rust and ruin, now remain.
Silent waves, a mournful song,
Whispers of where they belong.

Moonlight tips on crested waves,
Illuminates forgotten graves.
Anchors drift, a distant call,
Echoes lost, as shadows fall.

Salt and sea, they intertwine,
Bitter brine and fleeting time.
Chains unwind in twilight's fade,
Adrift they go, hearts betrayed.

Once were strong, now shadows gleam,
Anchors adrift through life's dream.
Tides of time, they ebb and flow,
Anchored souls, lost long ago.

The Silent Betrayer

Silent shadows in the night,
Whispered secrets kept from sight.
Trust's foundation starts to shake,
In silence, bonds begin to break.

Eyes that once conveyed delight,
Now are veiled in ghostly light.
Words unspoken, cold as ice,
Silent vows, a grave device.

Beneath the cloak of quietude,
Lurks betrayal's dark-mood.
Promises once strong and sheer,
Turn to whispers filled with fear.

Unseen rifts in hearts so still,
Silent acts, they start to kill.
Trust no longer holds the steel,
Silent deeds, the truth reveal.

Betrayer speaks not of the crime,
Yet it echoes through all time.
Silent once, the deed's betrayed,
In silence, trust too has swayed.

Fractured Alliance

Once we stood with bonds so tight,
Together faced the darkest night.
In unity, our strength was found,
Till fractures broke our sacred ground.

Cracks appeared in whispered cords,
Breaking under heavy swords.
Words that once were oaths of trust,
Turned to ashes, lost in dust.

Eyes that gleamed with shared intent,
Now with coldness, rage is spent.
Lines are drawn in shifting sands,
Grasp slips from united hands.

Promises like brittle glass,
Shattered on the paths we pass.
Joined in hope, now split apart,
Fractured pieces, broken hearts.

Past allegiance, torn and frayed,
Ghosts of what we once portrayed.
Alliance fractured, hearts in rift,
Bound and severed, lost adrift.

Mirror's Lies

Mirror's surface, cold and clear,
Reflects the lies we hold dear,
Shows the truth we want to see,
Fickle panes of what might be.

Eyes that gaze into the pane,
Seek the solace, hide the pain.
Mirror's whisper, soft deceit,
Twists the shadows at our feet.

Truth and falsehood intertwine,
Illusions bold, yet so benign.
Mirror, mirror, on the wall,
Hides the secrets in its thrall.

Shifting light and shadows play,
Lie and truth in disarray.
Gaze into the mirrored face,
Find the lies in its embrace.

Truth once hidden, now revealed,
In the glass, the truth concealed.
Mirror's lies, they fade away,
Leaving truths in open day.

The Broken Code

In circuits cold, a shiver lies
Where once did flow the spark of light
Beneath the darkened, clouded skies
The silence reigns, by day and night

A glitch has whispered in the wire
Trust, once strong, now frayed and torn
In binary fields of lost desire
A digital soul left forlorn

Echoes of commands, unspoken dreams
Are trapped within the silicon veins
A prisoner of forgotten schemes
In unraveling code, the spirit wanes

Restoring hope, a distant goal
When data trails to shadows fade
To mend the breach within the scroll
And piece by piece, the trust once laid

A silent quest to seek repair
In labyrinths of ones and zeros
For in the code, the heart laid bare
Will rise again, as techno-heroes

Silent Judgement

In eyes that cast a stedfast stare
Lies judgments spoken not aloud
A gaze dissecting, unaware
The weight it bears, its stealthy shroud

Whispers in the mind do grow
Where lips remain in quiet repose
The unvoiced verdicts ebb and flow
A tidal force that no one knows

In meetings hall, in crowded space
The silence speaks in subtle flair
A world within, a hidden place
Of justice rendered in mid-air

The heart perceives, yet cannot fight
The whispers faded in between
As shadows play in pale moonlight
The echoes of a silent screen

Though judgment seems to silent be
Its power stays, a lasting mark
In shadows long, in minds set free
A language of the silent dark

The Unfaithful Heart

Beneath the vows, a secret lies
A flicker in unfaithful flame
Where love once bloomed, now passion dies
And trust is lost in lover's name

Deceit, a whisper in the night
Soft steps on paths of reckless chase
The heart that roams is out of sight
Yet leaves behind a wounded trace

In shadows deep, the truth does melt
A bitter tale of love's demise
The faithful heart's unwavering pelt
Betrayed by lies and alibis

Amidst the tears, a strength will rise
To mend the wounds of trust betrayed
A heart once broken, yet so wise
Will heal in time, though love is frayed

The unfaithful heart, a caution tale
Of loyalty and broken chains
In time, the truth will tip the scale
And love will find its way through pains

Disguised Sorrow

A smile conceals the deepest woe
In eyes that glisten, tears take flight
Behind the mask, the sorrow flows
In darkness masked, escaping light

The laughter rings, so pure and clear
Yet shadows dance in hidden pain
The heart that weeps, in silence, near
Finds solace nowhere, but in rain

In masquerades of joyful pretense
The soul seeks refuge from the ache
A fragile act of false defense
To hide the cracks where spirits break

In quiet nights, the sorrow breathes
Unveiling truths beneath the guise
In solitude, the spirit heaves
To free the tears from captive eyes

And when the dawn of truth does rise
The mask will fall, the sorrow shown
Through open wounds, and heartfelt cries
A journey starts to heal alone

Deception's Dance

In twilight's haze we waltz, concealed,
A masquerade where truths are veiled.
We smile with secrets, hearts encased,
In shadows' grasp, our souls displaced.

A silent rhythm, steps entwined,
Yet lies and laughter intertwined.
We tango close in guarded trance,
Forever lost in deception's dance.

The music swells, a haunting grace,
Reflections hidden, face to face.
Each twirl and turn, a crafted chance,
Bound together in this dance.

Eyes meet, revealing half the tale,
A flicker where our masks prevail.
In fleeting glances, fate's advance,
Forever bound by deception's dance.

The final note, a ghostly sound,
In stillness, secrets are unwound.
We part with shadows, no second glance,
Escaping from deception's dance.

The Hidden Rift

Beneath the surface, tension vies,
A chasm deep where silence lies.
Between the words, where shadows drift,
We tiptoe 'round the hidden rift.

In quiet moments, echoes break,
Revealing cracks the heart can't fake.
Each whispered doubt, a hidden lift,
Etching lines through the hidden rift.

The daylight masks our unseen tears,
A facade built through countless years.
Yet in the night, with courage swift,
We face the truth of the hidden rift.

Though bridges fall, and ties may sever,
We hold to dreams of "forever."
In love's embrace, our spirits shift,
But still we fear the hidden rift.

To mend the wounds that cut so deep,
We cast aside the fears we keep.
Together strong, minds can uplift,
And heal the scars of the hidden rift.

The Forgotten Oath

In ancient halls where echoes sigh,
A vow was sworn beneath the sky.
Through ages lost in time's embrace,
An oath forgotten, left to trace.

Beneath the stars, a promise made,
In whispered winds, it starts to fade.
Through moonlit nights, a silent wraith,
The forgotten oath, a whispered faith.

In shadows deep, where memories sleep,
The echoes of our promise creep.
With every dawn, we search and grope,
For fragments of our broken hope.

Yet in our hearts, the fire burns,
For what we've lost, the spirit yearns.
Through tears and trials, we retrain,
To find the pledge we made in vain.

The path to truth, so rarely straight,
But in the end, it's never late.
To resurrect, with newfound growth,
The sacred bond of the forgotten oath.

Heartache's Whisper

In midnight's calm, where sorrows speak,
The heartache's whisper, soft and bleak.
A fragile breath, a tear-stained trace,
The memory of a tender grace.

Through nights of solitude, we roam,
In search of solace, far from home.
The echo of a love once bright,
Now shadows cast in pale moonlight.

With every sigh, we touch the past,
The moments fleeting, gone too fast.
Yet in the stillness, soft and true,
The heartache's whisper calls to you.

In dreams, we dance with spirits old,
And tales of love and loss unfold.
A tender voice, a touch so light,
In whispers carried through the night.

Though heartache lingers, soft and low,
Its gentle murmur helps us grow.
For in its pain, we find our will,
To love again, and cherish still.

The Faithless Promise

In twilight's tender, waning light,
A pledge was made, both pure and bright,
Yet quick as shadows shift and play,
The vow dissolved with break of day.

A heart once bound by earnest ties,
Now cast adrift in silent sighs,
The words once sweet, now void and pale,
Lost promises in whispers frail.

A faithless whisper 'neath the stars,
Brought forth a heart with countless scars,
In dreams, the echoes still resound,
An oath once lost, nowhere found.

For every promise turned to dust,
A memory forged in fragile trust,
In empty night, the truth unfurls,
The fleeting vows of faithless worlds.

Regret, a shadow by my side,
Echoes of promises denied,
Yet in the dawn, a hope renews,
A heart now strong, to seek what's true.

Cloaked in Kindness

A gentle touch, a tender gaze,
In kindness' light, we found our ways,
A cloak of solace, warm embrace,
In every glance, a soft grace.

With words unsaid, yet understood,
Healed by acts in quiet good,
Through trials met, we stood as one,
A bond of hearts, with kindness spun.

In shadows cast by days of grey,
The light within did gently sway,
For kindness shines, a guiding star,
Beyond the trials, near and far.

When sorrows seep and tears fall free,
A kind word whispers, 'Come to me',
In kindness' arms, we find our rest,
In simple acts, we're truly blessed.

A cloak of kindness, ever near,
Protects from harm, dispels the fear,
In hearts that sing a gentle song,
In kindness' embrace, we belong.

The Echo of Betrayal

A silent step, a whispered lie,
In shadows deep, the truth did die,
An echo of betrayal's sting,
A broken heart, no more to sing.

When trust was shattered, shards did fall,
A binding love turned cold and small,
In whispered winds, the secrets lay,
The echoes haunt both night and day.

The friendship forged in fires bright,
Extinguished now in darkened light,
As echoes of the past reveal,
The sting of wounds that never heal.

A trust once pure, now lost in time,
Betrayal's echo, haunting rhyme,
In every word, in every glance,
The broken bond, a mournful dance.

Yet from the ashes, strength may rise,
A heart renewed beneath the skies,
Though echoes linger, fade they might,
In time and truth, we find our light.

Crumbling Loyalty

A tower high, of trust and care,
Now crumbling slow in disrepair,
Each stone once strong, now frail and weak,
The cracks reveal the words we speak.

In moments lost, the truth unfolds,
A loyalty no longer bold,
The bonds once tight, now frayed and thin,
A silent end, as fault lines grin.

The heart's domain of love once sure,
Now questions what it can endure,
In quiet echoes, doubts arise,
As loyalty in silence dies.

Promises once steel and sure,
Now fade to myths we can't endure,
In quiet night, the whispers swell,
Of crumbling walls where loved ones fell.

Yet in the rubble, seeds may grow,
A new foundation, firm and slow,
From crumbling loyalty, we find,
A path to heal, rebuild, and bind.

Fading Loyalty

In days gone by, our bond was steel,
Steadfast hearts, with hands to feel,
Yet whispers grew, like autumn leaves,
That flutter down past hopes and grieves.

With every sunset, trust grew thin,
Echoes faded, from where we've been,
What once was golden, now turns gray,
As loyalty fades with each new day.

Eyes diverted, gazes cold,
Promises lost, stories old,
A silent drift from shore to shore,
Fading loyalty, forevermore.

Dust on memories, light grows dim,
Once synchronized, now out on a whim,
The ties that bind begin to fray,
Loyalty lost in the fray.

Yet ember glows in heart's deep core,
Yearning for what was once more,
A fleeting hope, a passion's plea,
In fading loyalty, might we be free?

Heart's Treachery

A whispered doubt, a shadowed glance,
Betrayal blooms in love's own dance,
What seems so true may fall apart,
Under the weight of a doubting heart.

Promises made in moonlit nights,
Now feel like knives in the daylight,
The heart, it weaves a tangled skein,
Of treachery mixed with love and pain.

Lies like venom, sweet and low,
Erode the foundations we used to know,
Deceit is but a gentle touch,
That steals trust, leaves us in clutch.

Through veils of tears, a truth we plea,
Does heart's treachery set us free?
Or bind us in a web of woe,
Where truth and falsehood ebb and flow?

Yet even in this stormy sea,
Might love break through and let us see,
That in the end, despite the scars,
Heart's treachery defines who we are.

The Masked Truth

Behind the smile, shadows play,
Hiding words we cannot say,
A masquerade of peace we've donned,
Truth concealed, for it's far gone.

What lies beneath, none can see,
A world of masked reality,
The face we show, a clever ruse,
To cover wounds that words abuse.

Eyes like mirrors, they reflect,
A heart that hides in self-protect,
Through layers thick, the truth is veiled,
A silent scream that has prevailed.

In secret corners, shadows grow,
Masked truth, we fear to show,
A guarded guard, a solemn pact,
To keep the pain from fighting back.

Yet somewhere deep within the core,
The masked truth yearns for more,
A hope that someday light will break,
And free the heart from each mistake.

Unwritten Scars

In silence deep, the scars reside,
Unwritten tales, where pain's applied,
Beneath the surface, where none see,
They whisper secrets, haunting me.

Touches that never leave a mark,
Yet in the heart, forever spark,
Wounds of the soul, no bandage meets,
In quiet nights, the trauma greets.

The ink of sorrow, staining time,
Each unwritten scar, in rhythm and rhyme,
Invisible chains that bind us tight,
In daylight's glare and darkest night.

Eyes may gleam with joyful light,
Hiding battles fought each night,
Unwritten scars, a silent tale,
Of endurance where words fail.

Yet in these scars, strength is born,
For every night, there's a dawn,
Unwritten scars pave paths unseen,
In those depths, the heart is keen.

The Blurred Line

Shadows dance where light should reign,
Truth and lies begin to wane,
A tightrope walk on shifting ground,
In foggy realms, what's lost is found.

Promises in whispered tones,
Speak to hearts, and chilled to bones,
Deeds and dreams, they intertwine,
In the space of the blurred line.

Hope and fear, both play their part,
In the theater of the heart,
Steps unsure, yet forward pressed,
Seeking peace in simple rest.

Colours merge where borders fade,
In twilight's soft cascade,
Bold and faint, in tandem, lie,
Beneath the ever-changing sky.

Balance tips with each new stride,
In shadows where the truths reside,
Trust must find its way again,
To see the line that once was plain.

Forked Tongues

Whispers in the moonlit night,
Where shadows stretch and take their flight,
Coiled serpents, silent and sly,
Forked tongues weave their silent lie.

Words like silk, but sharp as steel,
Beneath their weight, the truths conceal,
Intentions hidden, masked in grace,
Deception's art in every space.

Promises made with double edge,
From lush green grass to crumbling hedge,
In every heart, a doubt's seed sown,
A trust betrayed, yet seldom shown.

Sweet yet bitter, the tang of lies,
Gleam like stars in darkened skies,
Lines once pure, now tainted grey,
In silence, trust begins to fray.

In shadows dark where serpents dwell,
Silently weaves their twisted spell,
Be wary of the whispers heard,
For lies can latch to every word.

The Hidden Serpent

In gardens lush with flowers fair,
An unseen danger lingers there,
Beneath the blooms and verdant green,
A serpent lies, its form unseen.

It slithers low where eyes can't see,
A shadow's blur, swift and free,
In silence, it observes the world,
In coiled repose, its power unfurled.

With every step, a watchful gaze,
It glides through life's intricate maze,
Unseen, unknown, its presence felt,
A mystery in the hand is dealt.

The innocent and wise alike,
Can fall beneath its subtle strike,
Trust the flowers, but heed the vine,
Where serpent's secrets intertwine.

Though hidden deep, it bides its time,
In every tale and every rhyme,
A lesson cloaked in nature's art,
The hidden serpent guards its heart.

The Ruined Trust

In quiet moments, broken dreams,
A fractured heart, with silent screams,
Promises like shattered glass,
Trust once strong, now fades to past.

Spoken words like gentle breeze,
Turn to storms with angry seas,
A bond once held in purest light,
Now dims within the darkest night.

Eyes that once could see so clear,
Now blurred by doubt, by pain and fear,
Each whispered vow, a haunting ghost,
In minds, where betrayal boasts.

Healing slow, the scar's mark,
In memory's echo, shadows hark,
Yet hope may rise within the dust,
From the ashes of ruined trust.

Time may mend what once was torn,
In resilience, new faith is born,
Though trust once shattered, now seems lost,
Love may bloom despite the cost.

Smiles That Stain

Beneath the sunlit skies, they gleam
A mask we wear in life's cruel scheme
Behind the warmth, a chilling pain
Those brightened curves, mere smiles that stain

The laughter echoes, hollow, cold
A hidden truth in tales retold
While joy's pretense, on faces lain
Veils inner storms, with smiles that stain

In crowds we blend, with hearts concealed
Our vulnerable selves, never revealed
As shadows dance in joy's domain
We paint the world with smiles that stain

Our sorrows' depths remain unspoken
Behind a grin, our spirits broken
In life's charade, the moments feign
The happiness, those smiles that stain

The Unspoken Rift

A silence echoed through the hall
Between us stood an unseen wall
The words we feared were out of sight
In quiet hearts, the rift took flight

In whispered glances, secrets kept
Our anguished souls in darkness wept
No bridge to span the chasm's drift
The void, it grew, the unspoken rift

Time's cruel passage deepened scars
We drifted, guided by distant stars
A tapestry, by sorrow's hand did lift
Entangled lives in the unspoken rift

Through stormy nights and tear-filled days
The silence stayed, our bond decays
In shadows now our hearts did sift
For what was lost, the unspoken rift

Shadows of Pretend

Beyond the veil of acted roles
Lie weary hearts and burdened souls
Through masks we wear, our truth we fend
In life we dance, shadows of pretend

A fleeting flash, a staged delight
We claim our joy, by moon's pale light
Yet in the dark, our fears descend
Unseen by all, shadows of pretend

In moments brief, the truth revealed
Our feelings raw, no longer sealed
But dawn returns, illusions mend
Resuming once more, shadows of pretend

The world demands we play our part
To hide the grief within our heart
Each step we take, we can't defend
The fragile seams, shadows of pretend

The Fragile Trust

In bonds of faith, we place our hope
A delicate dance on a tightened rope
With whispered vows, in loves we trust
We walk the line, the fragile trust

One misstep and the ties may break
A single doubt, all trust can shake
In hearts it lives, both strong and just
Yet easily shattered, the fragile trust

Promises made, and secrets shared
A realm of truths that must be aired
Yet one betrayal, and comes the gust
The winds that sweep the fragile trust

With courage bound, our fears we face
On faith we tread, in tender grace
United souls in life's robust
Yet ever wary, the fragile trust

Masks of Deceit

In the shadows of the night
Where true faces lie in wait
Masks of deceit take their flight
Veiling souls, sealing fate

Eyes that glint with veiled intent
Lips that curve, yet never smile
Every promise, every scent
Crafting tales to beguile

In the daylight, shadows fade
Yet the mask remains in place
Truth and lies in a parade
Lines between them interlace

Whispers soft as summer breeze
Memories that twist and twine
Woven threads of silent pleas
Secrets held in hearts' confine

Through the masquerade we tread
Seeking truth behind disguise
Paths of gold and ones blood-red
Lost in masks, in woven lies

Faith Torn Asunder

In the chapel of one's heart
Where light and shadows dwell
Faith once strong, begins to part
In the silence, truths compel

Whispers echo off the walls
Solemn prayers now lost, confused
Faith shattered, as hope falls
Trust once whole, now bruised

Hands once clasped in reverent grace
Now fumble, seeking, yet unsure
In a world devoid of place
Searching for a cure

Tears of sorrow gently flow
Like rivers to a restless sea
Prophets from long ago
Echoing the plea

Rebuilding trust in time's embrace
From fragments scattered on the floor
Faith renews in subtle grace
Stronger than before

Secrets and Scars

Behind smiles, the stories hide
Wounds and whispers left to heal
Secrets kept so deep inside
Even hearts dare not reveal

Tales of love and loss entwined
Etched in flesh and soul alike
Scars that guard the fragile mind
In their silent, endless strike

Beneath the laughter, traces show
Paths of sorrow, lines of pain
Silent echoes, whispers low
Bound within, like iron chains

Yet from scars, new strength does grow
Lessons learned and wisdom gained
In resilience, hearts bestow
Hope revived and unrestrained

Through the valleys dark and deep
With each step, we redefine
From our secrets, scars we keep
Forms the essence of our sign

Whispers of Deceit

In the stillness of the night
Whispers weave a tangled net
Truths are shrouded, lost from sight
Promises that breed regret

Voice so soft, yet sharp as steel
Spins the tale of false intent
In the shadows, lies conceal
What the heart would not prevent

Secrets murmured in the dark
Carried on the breath of fate
Each deception leaves its mark
Twining paths of love and hate

Eyes that gaze through veils of mist
Seeking glimpses of the core
Of the truths that once were kissed
Now obscured forevermore

In the dance of light and shade
Whispers guide the steps we meet
In this masquerade we've played
Led by whispers of deceit

Lies in the Breath

In whispers soft as velvet shrouds,
Untruths weave through the misty air.
Promises light as fleeting clouds,
Dissolve, and truth grows ever rare.

Deceptive words with silver sheen,
Mask intentions hidden deep.
Each phrase, a ghost unseen,
Waking dreams from darkest sleep.

The breaths of lies paint twilight hues,
On the canvas of our faith.
Shadows consume the morning dews,
Leaving trust in fragile state.

With every sigh and silent pause,
Falsehood claims the night and day.
We grapple with deceitful claws,
In realms where truth's harsh light won't stay.

In this mist our hearts do tread,
Seeking light where lies have bled.

Broken Oaths

A whispered promise, softly sealed,
Rings through the corridors of time.
Yet bonds once strong and tightly healed,
Can fall to dust, a solemn crime.

With every oath that breaks apart,
Echoes of trust in silence ring.
A scar imprinted on the heart,
Where once a loyal tune did sing.

Each shattered vow, a shattered dream,
Each broken word, a breaking wave.
In hearts where silent sorrows scream,
And shadowed memories we crave.

The fragments of our pledge remain,
Among the ruins of our past.
A bitter taste, a blunt refrain,
Of promises that could not last.

Yet 'midst the wreckage, hope may rise,
A future built on clearer skies.

The Promise Breaker

In shadows where the echoes lay,
A promise never meant to hold.
The words once bright, now dull and gray,
Turn hope and dreams to barren cold.

With velvet tongue and charming guise,
The promise breaker weaves the tale.
Each whisper lined with soft disguise,
As honesty begins to pale.

Promises, like fragile glass,
Shatter with the lightest touch.
Future hopes, now memories past,
Of trust once held, now hurt so much.

In every heart where trust was laid,
The seeds of doubt start to grow.
The promise breaker's cruel charade,
Leaves wounds that time heals slow.

Yet still within the wreckage, gleams,
The fragile light of newer dreams.

Untrustworthy Smiles

Behind the curve of lips so fine,
A secret shadow starts to climb,
Echoes hide, deceit entwines,
Whispers lost in webs of time.

Eyes that sparkle, lies concealed,
Promises that fate repealed,
In the quiet, truths revealed,
Fragile hearts left unhealed.

Gentle laughs with sharpened thorns,
Hallowed words that twist and mourn,
Innocence forever torn,
Dreams betrayed by life's sworn storms.

Patterns shift in wicked ways,
Trust, a pawn in shadowed plays,
Hope dissolves in muted grays,
Untrustworthy smiles decay.

Fading light, a silent plea,
Masked intentions, none foresee,
Boundaries lost in mystery,
Fragments of what used to be.

The Trickster's Gaze

In eyes that glint with hidden fire,
Lies a maze of sweet desire,
Deftly spun, the heart retires,
Caught within that gaze, entire.

Mirrors dance with shifting shade,
Promises that softly fade,
Truths that once were clear, now swayed,
All beneath the trickster's blade.

Laughter whispers, shadows play,
Through the night and into day,
Words that lead the heart astray,
In the trickster's gaze, we stay.

Bound by wonder, tricked by light,
Lost within the endless night,
In the gaze where wrong feels right,
Held by charm and fleeting sight.

Waking dreams and silent cries,
Echoes of deceptive ties,
Caught within the trickster's lies,
In the gaze where freedom dies.

The Weakening Bond

Once, our hearts beat strong in sync,
Shared visions in the twilight's brink,
Now the ties begin to sink,
In the waning, we rethink.

Words once fluent now run dry,
Silent gaps replace the sky,
Eyes that met now question why,
In the bond that we let lie.

Distance grows in unseen ways,
Memories start to drift and fade,
In the shadows, futures fray,
In the weakening bond, we stay.

Echoes of what used to be,
Fragile hopes in shattered plea,
Dreams dissolve in entropy,
Anchor lost in endless sea.

Through the cracks, our hearts do fall,
Echoes bounce off hollow walls,
In this bond, we stand so small,
Waiting for the final call.

Mysteries Unveiled

Within the veil of night's embrace,
Lies a realm where shadows chase,
Through the dark, the stars replace,
Whispers of a hidden grace.

Secrets murmured in the breeze,
Linger in the bending trees,
Mysteries that bring unease,
Stories that the silence frees.

Ancient echoes fill the air,
Tales of magic, whispers rare,
In the night, we pause to care,
Seeking truths we scarcely dare.

Paths unfolding, fog descends,
Journeys where the mind extends,
In the veil, where time suspends,
Mysteries that never end.

Eyes alight with newfound sight,
Dreams unveiled in moonlit night,
Through the dark, we seek the light,
Mysteries revealed in flight.

9 789916 756164